Different Like Confetti

written by Larissa Grabois

illustrated by Adrian Curti
2020

D1560496

"We all have different gifts, so we
all have different ways of saying
to the world who we are."

~Fred Rogers
Mister Rogers' Neighborhood

Different Like Confetti
This is Who I Am: Kids Empowerment Series, Book 2

Bill is a middle schooler, who faces everyday challenges in school due to a learning disability. In this book, the author Larissa Grabois helps Bill express his feelings and frustrations: "Trust me, it can get real tough, breezing through a school day in a huff" and "I feel like I'm walking on thin beams, and making friends and keeping them, is harder than it seems". Although this poem's message may provoke empathy, young readers will learn that despite his challenges, Bill has his own unique talents and gifts. This book, illustrated with humility by a high school sophomore Adrian Curti, aims to encourage kids to embrace all kinds of differences among their peers and in themselves. Bill tries to teach us that each and every one has something valuable to offer, if we just stop and notice. 'Different Like Confetti' is also available as an original song.

Contents:

* 'Different Like Confetti', an illustrated poem
* 'Different Like Confetti' interactive activity pages
* About the Author
* About the Artist
* 'Different Like Confetti' song on major music platforms

Project and creative design consultation by Dr. Irina Perelman

Graphic book design by Larissa Grabois

text, music and illustrations (c) 2020 Larissa Grabois

Self published by KDP Amazon
ISBN: 979-8-5757-1714-0

Weblinks are of a dynamic nature and may change over time.
Contact the author for more information if changes occur and for bulk book orders
at www.larissagmusic.info

"Last week I met a boy named Bill.

Bill told me he has trouble in school, because he cannot sit still!

So together, we wrote a song about what Bill wanted to spill..."

Larissa Grabois

Download our song 'Different Like Confetti' ♪ on all major music platforms!!! ♪

Have you ever wondered why?

We are all so different, you and I?

Tall or short, sad or happy,
shy or chatty?

We are all so different,
so colorful,

just like confetti!!

Some touch to read the letters,

others lean on a cane to walk.

While some others were not given,

the precious gift,

the luck,

to sing or talk.

Have you ever wondered why?

Some folks do well in all they try?

I myself,
I struggle,
have a hard time, with a lot.

Whether trying, trying hard

real hard or not!

Not everybody,
is equally
strong or smart!

But if you try,
to take a look at them
with your heart.

Though they may not be
the best
in what they do.

They're blessed with
their unique gifts,
their special gifts,
like me and you!

So please,
can you take a step
and try?

To stop and notice me
when I'm passing by?

I'll show you things,
that no one knew!

The unique things,
the cool things

that I can do!

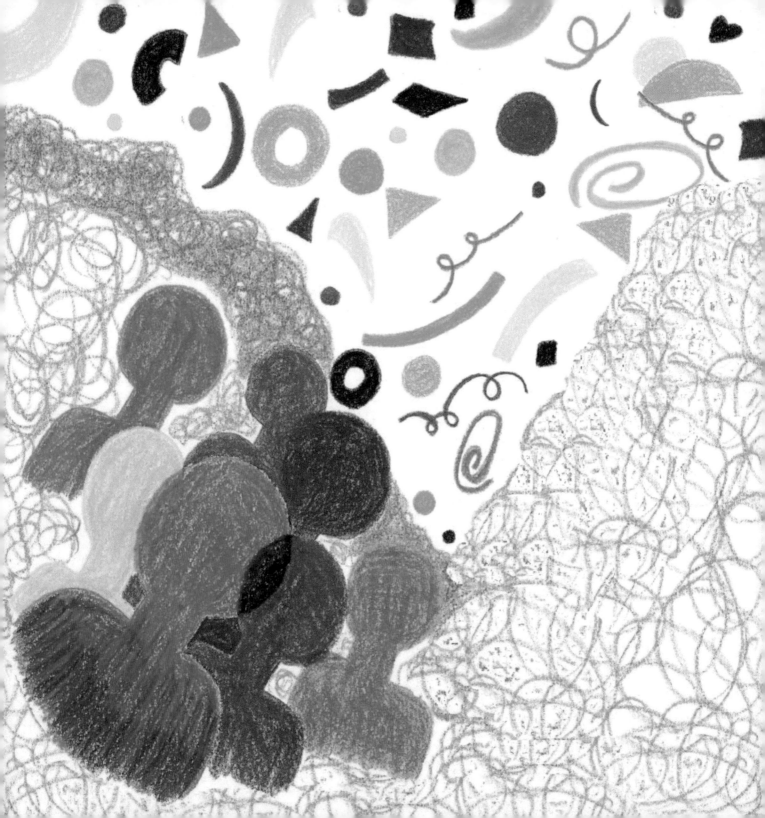

My list of things that make me special and different:

_____

_____

_____

_____

_____

_____

_____

_____

_____

_____

We all have different interests and abilities! Everyone is good at something!

When you grow up, what would you like to do?
Circle ANY number of items,
and compare with siblings, classmates, or friends

Soccer Player   Musician   Engineer   Teacher   Chef

Nurse   Book Author   Tennis Player   Police Officer

Firefighter   Dentist   Singer   Builder   Hairdresser

Football Player   Artist   Car Mechanic   Poet   Pilot   Nanny

Dancer   Plumber   Doctor   Mailman   Songwriter   Bus Driver

Basketball Player   Scientist   Truck Driver   Actor/Actress

Ship Captain   Hockey Player   Garden Worker   Train Engineer

Computer Scientist   Veterinarian Worker   Baseball Player

We are all different like confetti!
Draw your own confetti of any
size or shape that you can imagine...

We are all different like confetti!
Keep on drawing...

About the Author

Larissa Grabois is an inspirational book author
for both children and adults, a songwriter and a musician.

Larissa's book themes and
songwriting genre are inspired
by her childhood growing up
on the autism spectrum. The topics of
Larissa's books range from autism and
disability awareness to encouragement
of self-confidence, positive thinking
and overcoming challenges. Larissa aims
to captivate her readers and listeners
in a unique and emotionally engaging
fashion- through illustrated poems and
stories, offered at the same time in a
form of original songs and musical
compositions, which readers can follow
while reading the books. In fulfilling
her dream of transforming her
musical projects to a book format,
Larissa decided to feature high school
art students from her hometown
of Leonia, NJ as the illustrators of her
books in the summer of 2020, during
the coronavirus quarantine.

A performing singer and pianist, with a repertoire of songs
in multiple languages and musical genres, Larissa also holds
a 2017 MT-BA degree in Music Therapy with honors
from Montclair State University, NJ which in turn, also shaped
her path as an inspirational author and a composer.

About the Artist

Adrian Curti was selected by Larissa Grabois to illustrate 'Different Like Confetti' from a pool of several other artists, because she felt his art style and imagination would suit the theme of this book. Adrian, who is a Leonia artist, illustrated 'Different Like Confetti' at the age of 16 over the summer of 2020, during the coronavirus quarantine.

"I've been doing art for most of my life and it's been a great opportunity to be 16 years old and illustrate a book. Although I have never illustrated anything of this nature, I think the drawings came out very well for the two-month period I had to do it. I feel like I owe my versatility as an artist in part to the Leonia High School Arts Academy, which inspired me to be even more in touch with my ambition to become an artist".

~Adrian Curti

Other Works by this Author:

Shy Am I

includes
coloring pages
and
♪ a link to 'Shy Am I' song ♪

Written and illustrated by
Larissa Grabois   Mitchell Tonelson
Irina Perelman
Original story by Judi Weinberger

Download the song 'I Can Do It Myself'
and coloring pages!!!

I CAN DO IT
MYSELF

a book put to music by
Larissa Grabois, Mitchell Tonelson and Irina Perelman
Original story by Judi Weinberger

MY NAME IS
FAYE

Written by
Larissa G.   Illustrated by
Donovan H.

Don't
Forget
that
LIFE ROCKS!

written by Larissa Grabois
illustrated by Elie Whang
includes a link to the song 'Don't Forget that Life Rocks'

all books by Larissa Grabois can be purchased on Amazon
with accompanying music tracks available for download
on major music platforms

Made in the USA
Middletown, DE
06 January 2023

21251747R00015